TEA LEAF READING

DEBORAH ASHE

DEDICATION

To the Grouchy One

CONTENTS

ACKNOWLEDGMENTS

To everyone who has ever been filled with wonder and
awe.

To all those who have visited with me to learn their futures
and to all those who did not believe.

1 THE FUTURE

Is the future there in your teacup? Perhaps. Have you looked? Tea Leaf Reading has a long and varied history. From the fun get together of a few friends to the serious and introspective visit to a professional reader, each experience is fascinating and enlightening. For the novice, the main advice I have is to just enjoy the process. There's no wrong way to learn. Get your friends together and practice on them. What could be more fun than tea and fortune telling instead of the usual coffee klatch?

As long as there have been people, there have been those who seek to foretell the future. From oracles to fortune tellers, there are those that see and there are those that seek. Many folks will visit a fortune teller to try and unravel the mysteries beyond the veil. The laughter, the doubts, the testing questions and the intake of breath when a revelation hits home, are all part of the delightful ritual that is Tea Leaf Reading.

There are many ways to scry what might be and what to prepare yourself for. Most of these ways take years of practice and vary with individual skills. From reading the cards to interpreting omens and portents, we all love to hear stories of prophecy and possibilities.

Tea Leaf Reading or Tasseography, is open to all those that wish to try their hand. All you need is some tea, a teacup and saucer, an open mind, a familiarity with symbols and some intuition.

This Little Book of Tea Leaf Reading is intended to aid you in learning to interpret the shapes and patterns left in the bottom of your teacup. Practice is the only skill you will need, as you train your mind to look closer and see the threads of fate that twine their way from leaf to leaf. Don't forget to relax and enjoy the process, it's not a test of your 'psychic' abilities or your talents, it's a fun and traditional way to share some time with others and glimpse a little of life together.

Whether you learn for fun or to seek hidden knowledge, the results are the same. A lot of fun with a frisson of the forbidden. Let's see what we can open up for you. Starting today you are a Tea Leaf Reader. Put the kettle on, get the tea ready, and let's go!

2 PREPARING TO READ

When you are preparing to read the leaves for another person you become the Reader and the Inquirer. The Inquirer has the questions to ask and will be the person who consumes the tea. The Reader is the person who will be interpreting the patterns and sequences. It's good practice to remove any personal opinions from your mind before you open yourself to the intuitive process of reading the leaves. This style of reading is very free form and you should find yourself seeing the patterns in no time, liken it to seeing forms in clouds

It is important to note that loose leaf tea is to be used and a smaller leaf is usually better for even distribution around the teacup. A larger leaf tea, such as a green tea that unfolds can be used but is less likely to form distinct patterns. I have always found that a black tea such as English Breakfast Tea has around the right grind for a good pattern making brew. Use what you have to hand and see what works for you.

There is no right or wrong way to do this, but with practice you will gain a preference for the size of tea leaf you prefer to work with. If all you have is tea in a tea bag, cut one open and use that. The grind will be very fine and powdery and not as pleasant to drink, but will still work for a reading.

Some good teas to start with.
- English Breakfast
- Irish Breakfast
- Orange Pekoe
- Earl Grey

For more advanced readings [larger leaf]
- Tulsi
- Gunpowder Green
- Mint Tea

The Cup

Shallow, with wide brim

The cup should be fairly shallow and have a wider top than bottom. A fluted or narrow topped cup won't be all that easy to see into. I usually use a divination cup that has patterns pre printed on it, but I don't always use those patterns to interpret the reading. The cup itself is perfect for the job and would be equally effective if it had no markings on it at all and was plain.

Alternatively, you could take a plain cup of the same shape and place markings there of your own devising. Past, present and future markings for instance. Make it work for you.

This is your divination tool and you should be comfortable with it, up to and including the colour and design of the cup. Make it part of your ritual.

Firstly, seeking out a suitable cup – at thrift stores, shops and vintage stores, or making your own. It's a great idea to have several cups and use the style and design that pertains to your reading at that time. Perhaps decorate one with a theme to match the questions. Hearts for relationship queries or cars, planes and trains for travel. There's no limit to your artistic intuitions. Beware of using themes for general readings as your mind will fill in the gaps.

Brewing the Tea

The Inquirer will drink their cup of tea in the normal manner and consume all but the liquid in the very bottom. Quite often the tea leaves have dropped to the bottom of the cup and it becomes unpleasant to drink the leaves down, so the Inquirer will naturally stop drinking at the ideal point. Around a teaspoon of liquid is usually enough for a good swirl. The main point of this being to allow the leaves to move freely around. Too dry and you'll just have clumps. Brewing properly helps here too, give the leaves time to soak up the water and unfurl to their full extent.

If there is a little much liquid left in the cup for your purposes, use the saucer to drain a little out without losing any of the leaves and leaving enough tea to 'swirl' the leaves around. Turn the cup the right way up again. This is to check that you have all the leaves and an ample supply of tea in the cup. If you feel this brew is not going to give you a good reading, simply start over. No one I know will object to a second cup of tea. If you serve biscuits or cookies with your tea, don't allow dunking because bits of cookie crumbles in the tea leaves are going to make forming patterns a little difficult.

The Inquirer should hold the cup in their left hand and gently swirl the leaves and liquid around. Lefthanded people can reverse the instructions. Your non dominant hand is connected to the spiritual realm and you should use that hand when asking spirit to communicate or to aid in foretelling the future. If you do reverse the hand that is being used,

Drink the Tea

it's a good idea to reverse the direction of the reading too. They should match.

Right handed person swirls with the left hand and reads cup from the right, clockwise. Left handed person swirls with the right hand

and reads cup from the handle at the left and reads anti clockwise.

Once you have swirled the tea around to the left 3 times, turn the cup upside down on the saucer to let the remaining liquid out and the tea leaves will stick to the drying cup.

It's traditional to turn the cup three times anti clockwise [while upside down] and now it's ready to be interpreted. I usually place the saucer upside down on top of the cup while it's the right way up, so that you can avoid spilling liquid and tea leaves all over you. Then simply turn the teacup and saucer over together. You'll develop your own way of achieving this in a smooth and professional manner. Think of how you upend a cake to remove from the baking tin, and you'll have it.

If you wish you may focus on the question being asked while the swirling of the tea is in progress, certainly it's a good practice to do so while turning the cup for the last time before reading. If the Inquirer wants to have a 'blind' reading wherein they don't share their question with you, then have them focus on their intent as they carry out the task.

Invert the Cup

When you first start reading, it's a great idea to have a small tray or cloth under your cup in case some of the tea spills out. This is nothing to worry about and will happen quite a lot when you are first practicing. It's a bit of a knack to swirl, tip and invert the cup and saucer while liquid is in it. Often the Inquirer will be a little nervous or excited and may drop the cup. Just clear up any spills and if there are enough leaves to read, continue. And if there are not enough leaves to read, make some more tea and start over.

Don't be too literal in your interpretations. Try to practice going with your first impressions. This is a very intuitive art and looking too hard and too scientifically can take away some of your instincts. If something reminds you of an

Elephant, it's to be seen as an Elephant. It doesn't have to be anatomically correct or proportional.

Think of the leaves as part of an impressionist painting. What do you see when you first glance in the cup. What pops out at you. Make a mental or physical note of your first thoughts when you peer into the patterns.

Go back over for a second look once you are happy with your first instincts. Are their connecting patterns? For instance; if you see a ring in the position of distant future and an anchor in the position of the present, is there a connecting travel symbol between the two? An airplane, a balloon, some straight lines? This is how you develop a basic interpretation into a more detailed look at the future. Take a third look for tiny patterns. You should talk through your findings as you make them and make the Inquirer part of the process. They will be delighted as they see their tea leaves reveal so many secrets.

3 THE READING

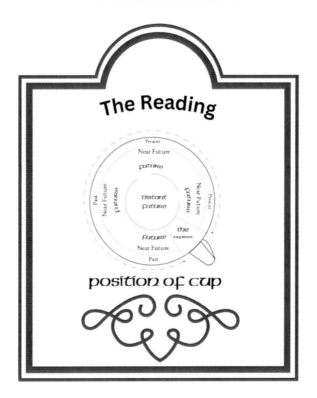

We will be using the Position of Cup diagram as the standard position for all your readings. If you always work from the handle to the right and read clockwise from the handle you will find it easier to become comfortable with your interpretations.

Keep this diagram in mind if you find you have to reverse the reading for a leftie. There's nothing wrong with keeping a diagram in front of you if it helps accustom you to your sequences.

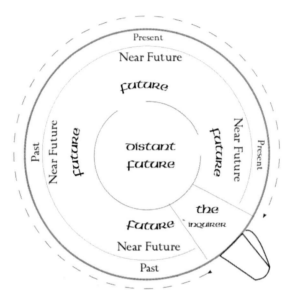

posítíon of cup

Use the worksheets at the end of the book to practice your readings. Once you are comfortable with your interpretations and positions of the symbols, you can start linking them together. If you have a digital copy of this book, just sketch some copies of the sheets on paper.

4 SYMBOLS

- Acorn: At top, slow growth; at bottom, good health. With a good omen; your perseverance will be rewarded. With a negative omen; you may be wasting your time on an unrewarding task.
- Airplane: Long journey; a rise in social position. Towards the inner cup; travel for work. Towards the outer rim; travel for enjoyment and recreation, vacation or honeymoon [if with rings]

- Anchor: At top, stability and rest; at bottom, safety. With a good omen; security and comfort. With a negative omen: boredom and becoming entrenched into a rut.
- Apple: Achievement; if bitten into, temptation.
- Arrow: Point down, bad news; up, good news.
- Axe: Difficulties; if at top, overcoming of difficulties.
- Baby: Fretting and small worries.

- Bag: A trap; if open, escape, from a trap. all: Variable fortune, as ball bounces up and down.
- Balloon: A celebration or party soon.
- Basket: A treat, award, compliment, recognition.
- Bell: Announcement; the nearer the top, the better.
- Birds: Good news (see also species of birds).
- Boat: A visit from a friend, protection, inheritance.

- Book: If open, good news; if closed, hidden secrets.
- Bottle: Drunkenness, temptations offered.
- Broom: A new home; a thorough house-cleaning.
- Bush: A secret friend or secret opportunities.
- Butterfly: Fickleness of friends.
- Candle: Ask for and receive help from others.
- Cat: Gossip; black, luck; cat-head, female false friend.

- Chain: Engagement, wedding; sequence of events.
- Chair: A guest is coming.
- Circle: Success, completion; with dots, a baby.
- Clock: Better health if medical help is sought soon.
- Clouds: Trouble; with dots (rain), many problems
- Coin: Money count the coins to tell how much.
- Cross: Death, a funeral, suffering, sacrifice.

- Cup: Reward of merit; overturned, justified criticism.

- Dagger: Danger from self or others; beware injury.

- Dish: Trouble at home; matters require cleaning up.

- Dog: Good, true friend; at bottom, friend needs help.

- Door: Opportunities arise through an odd event.

- Duck: Money, and false gossip about money.

- Eagle: Success by soaring over obstacles.
- Egg: If unbroken, success; if broken, failure.
- Envelope: Good news; with dots, news of money.
- Eye: Look sharp; be cautious; you may be psychic.
- Face: A change is coming. It may be a setback.
- Fan: Flirtation, but it comes to nothing in the end.

- Feather: Insincerity, undependability, lack of focus.
- Fence: Limitations, minor setbacks, easily mended.
- Finger: Extra emphasis on whatever it points to.
- Fire: At top, achievement; at bottom, danger, haste.
- Fish: Increase of wealth or increase in family.

- Flag: Danger if you compromise your integrity.
- Flower: Compliments, tokens of love and esteem.
- Fly: Domestic annoyances require your attention.
- Forked Line: You must soon make a decision.
- Fruit: Prosperity, a successful outcome to labour.

- Gate: Opportunity, future success beckons.
- Glass, Water: Integrity and temperance.
- Glass, Cocktail: Dissatisfaction with life.
- Goat: Beware stubborn people; they may be enemies.
- Grapes: Good health, fertility, happiness; inebriation.
- Gun: Anger, discord, strife; danger where it points.

- Hammer: Hard work is needed; avoid complainers.
- Hand: Open, a friendly helper; closed, an argument.
- Hat: Improvement, a new role or a new job.
- Hawk: Suspicion and jealousy; watch with care.
- Heart: Love, pleasure, romance, a thrilling meeting.
- Horse: Galloping, good news; head only, a lover.

- Horseshoe: Good luck, a winning bet, good fortune.
- Hourglass: You must decide something soon.
- House: Security and safety; parents.
- Insect: Minor problems require immediate attention.
- Jewels: Gifts will be offered to you.
- Kettle: Minor illness; don't worry; friends will help.
- Key: Success, prosperity, understanding.

- Kite: Ascent in social position by the help of friends.
- Knife: A broken friendship; a justified fear.
- Ladder: Job promotion, a rise in life, advancement.
- Lamp: At top, a feast; at side, secrets revealed.
- Leaf: Change in health: up, better; down, worse.

- Letter: News; If cross near, death, if coins, a gift.
- Lines: If straight, progress; if wavy, uncertain path.
- Lion: An influential friend in a position of authority.
- Lock: Obstacles too strong to overcome.
- Man: Near handle, a visitor; elsewhere, a pen-pal.
- Moon: A change in plans.

- Mountain: Great goals beset by difficulties.
- Mouse: Someone is stealing from you.
- Mushroom: At top, country life; at bottom, growth.
- Nail: Injustice, unfairness, unrighteous punishment.
- Necklace: Whole, admirers; broken, losing a lover.
- Nest: Save your money; take care of your home.

- Needle: Recognition, admiration.
- Oak Tree: Strength, health, long life; betterment.
- Octopus: Danger.
- Ostrich: Travel abroad.
- Owl: Gossip nearby; a wise person will protect you.
- Palm Tree: Success, honour.
- Palm Leaf: Victory, martyrdom.
- Parasol: A new lover.

- Parrot: Foreign journey; people talk about you.
- Pig: Greed and carelessness.
- Pin: A new job awaits.
- Pine Tree: High achievement.
- Pipe: Reconciliation of a friendship.
- Pistol: Danger is near.
- Plough: A struggle ahead; hard going.
- Purse: At top, profit; at bottom, loss.

- Question Mark: Be cautious; future unsettled.
- Rabbit: Bravery to overcome a fear of disaster.
- Rainbow: The most difficult time is now over.
- Rake: Watch details lest you stumble.
- Raven: Bad news; love disaster; death for the aged.

- Rider: Good news from afar, especially in finances.
- Ring: At top, marriage; at bottom, betrothal.
- Ring, Broken: Divorce or broken engagement.
- Rose: Popularity, romance.
- Scales: Balanced, justice; unbalanced, injustice.
- Scissors: Quarrels, possibly separation.

- Sheep: Good fortune; a friend does your bidding.
- Shell: Good news from over the sea.
- Ship: At top, a journey; at bottom, a safe journey.
- Shoe: Hard work leads to a change for the better.
- Sickle: Illness, sorrow, and pain.
- Snake: An enemy, and wisdom to discern who it is.

- Spider: Good luck, a reward for industrious work.

- Spoon: Generosity.

- Squirrel: Save up now for future times of want.

- Stairs: Orderly progress leads to eventual success.

- Star: Health, happiness, hope; absolute success.

- Sun: Joy, success, power, children, well-being.
- Sword: Small quarrels turn into serious arguments.
- Table: A social gathering at which you'll find favour.
- Teardrops: Sorrow and tears.
- Tent: Travel for which you are not well prepared.

- Thimble: Changes at home; a need for mending.
- Tortoise: Criticism, usually beneficial.
- Tower: Disappointment and possible ruin.
- Triangle: Something unexpected will happen.
- Turtle: Slow progress; a sluggard is near to you.
- Umbrella: Trouble, but you will be protected.

- Vase: A friend needs your help.
- Violin: A self-centered person.
- Volcano: Harmful and emotional words may erupt.
- Wagon: A wedding will ensue.
- Wasp: Your romantic problems are due to a rival.
- Wheel: If whole, good fortune; if broken, loss.
- Wings: Messages from Heaven.

- Wolf: Cunning and jealousy.

- Zebra: Adventures overseas.

5 WORK SHEETS

tea leaf reading

Sketch the images that you see and plot their position in the cup
- refer back as needed for further interpretation

Image	Time Frame
	Position
	Symbolism
	Notes:

Interpretation:

tea Leaf reaoing

Sketch the images that you see and plot their position in the cup
- refer back as needed for further interpretation

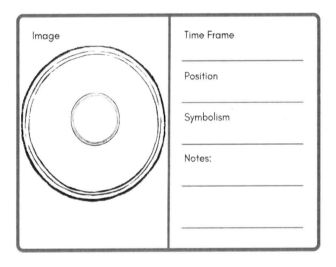

Interpretation:

tea leaf reading

Sketch the images that you see and plot their position in the cup
- refer back as needed for further interpretation

Image	Time Frame
	Position
	Symbolism
	Notes:

Interpretation:

tea leaf reading

Sketch the images that you see and plot their position in the cup
- refer back as needed for further interpretation

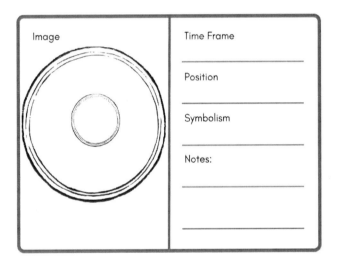

Image	Time Frame
	Position
	Symbolism
	Notes:

Interpretation:

tea Leaf Reading

Sketch the images that you see and plot their position in the cup
- refer back as needed for further interpretation

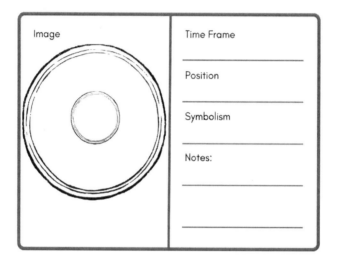

Image	Time Frame
	Position
	Symbolism
	Notes:

Interpretation:

tea leaf reading

Sketch the images that you see and plot their position in the cup
- refer back as needed for further interpretation

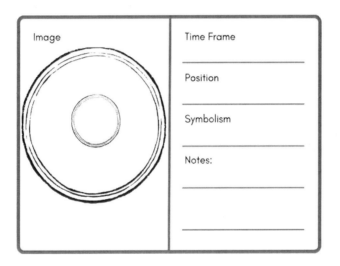

Image	Time Frame
	Position
	Symbolism
	Notes:

Interpretation:

tea leaf reaoing

Sketch the images that you see and plot their position in the cup
- refer back as needed for further interpretation

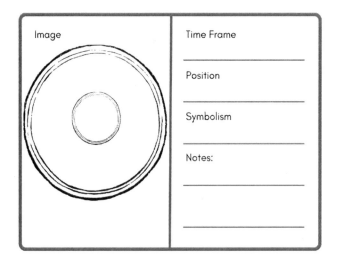

Interpretation:

tea leaf reading

Sketch the images that you see and plot their position in the cup
- refer back as needed for further interpretation

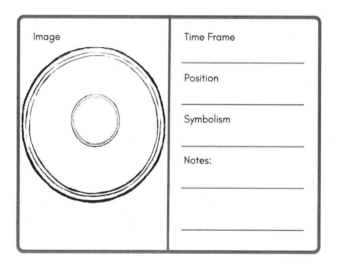

Image

Time Frame

Position

Symbolism

Notes:

Interpretation:

tea leaf reading

Sketch the images that you see and plot their position in the cup
- refer back as needed for further interpretation

Image	Time Frame
	Position
	Symbolism
	Notes:

Interpretation:

ABOUT THE AUTHOR

Deborah Ashe was born in England but has lived in the USA for the past 26 years. She currently resides in Tennessee with her husband, two dogs and 6 cats. She has 3 children, 2 bonus children, 3 Grandchildren and 1 Great Grandchild. She loves to grow her own food and has a small permaculture food garden which is well kept by Chickens and Ducks. She is the owner of Ten and Six Teas, a small artisan blend tea company that supplies hand made tea blends. For many years she read Tarot, Runes and Tea Leaves at local Renaissance Faires and Psychic Events and participated in many wellness activities as a Reiki and Meditation Coach.

Made in United States
Cleveland, OH
29 April 2025

16496483R00033